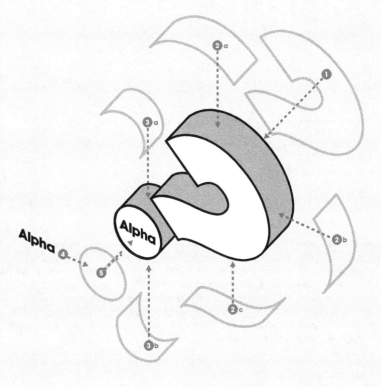

**RUN ALPHA
HANDBOOK**

Published in North America by Alpha North America, 1635 Emerson Lane, Naperville, IL 60540

© Alpha North America, 2017

Run Alpha Handbook

Printed in the United States of America

Unless otherwise noted, all Scripture in this publication is from the Holy Bible, New International Version (NIV), Copyright 1973, 1978, 1984, 2011 International Bible Society, used by permission of Zondervan. All rights reserved. *Holy Bible*, New Living Translation, copyright ©1996, 2004, 2015 by Tyndale House Foundation. Used by permission of Tyndale House Publishers, Inc., Carol Stream, Illinois 60188. All rights reserved. The New Testament in Modern English by J. B. Phillips copyright ©1960, 1972 J. B. Phillips. Administered by The Archbishops' Council of the Church of England. Used by permission. *Good News Translation (GNT)* Copyright ©1992 by American Bible Society.

ISBN 978-1-938328-95-4

1 2 3 4 5 6 7 8 9 10 Printing/Year 20 19 18 17

Contents

Fundamentals

What is Alpha?

Alpha is an opportunity to explore life and the Christian faith in a friendly, open and informal environment. It's run in churches, bars, coffee shops and homes worldwide. Essentially, Alpha is a safe place to explore life's biggest questions.

WHAT'S THE STORY?

Alpha started in 1977 in England, in a church called Holy Trinity Brompton, affectionately known as HTB. HTB was very theologically rooted and was using Alpha as a course for new Christians or those new to the church. In 1991, a young pastor named Nicky Gumbel took over leading Alpha and he observed that it was effective at connecting with people outside of the church. He noticed the general format and lack of pressure resonated with most people, but especially with young adults. At this time in England, and much of Europe, many assumptions about faith in God, the Bible and Jesus were being abandoned, similar to what we are experiencing in the US and Canada today.

People no longer assumed that God was true or that the Bible was trustworthy. Instead of asking if things were true, people were asking what was real. Nicky repositioned Alpha for non-churchgoers by replacing what was a small group Bible study with a time of discussion and an opportunity for people to ask questions and express their own views.

Alpha became highly relational and intentionally created a safe environment where people could share their opinions and points of view, no matter what they might be. Church leaders from around the world began asking how to run Alpha, and Nicky and the team at HTB passed on all they knew. The response has been overwhelming. Today, we estimate that over 30 million people have done Alpha globally.

WHEN ALPHA WORKS:

"And so it is with me, brothers and sisters. When I came to you I did not come with eloquence or human wisdom as I proclaimed to you the testimony about God. For I resolved to know nothing while I was with you except Jesus Christ and him crucified. I came to you in weakness with great fear and trembling. My message and my preaching were not with wise and persuasive words, but with a demonstration of the Spirit's power so that your faith might not rest on human wisdom, but on God's power."

1 Corinthians 2: 1-5

A TYPICAL ALPHA SESSION

Every Alpha session has three key elements: food, a talk and discussion:

FOOD

Whether it's a group of friends gathered around a kitchen table, or a quick catch-up over coffee and cake, food has a way of bringing people together. It's no different at Alpha. We start with food, because it's a great way to encourage community and get to know each other.

TALK

The talks are designed to engage and inspire conversation. Generally thirty minutes long, they can be given as a live talk or played as a video. They explore the big issues around faith and unpack the basics of Christianity, addressing questions such as Who is Jesus? and How can I have faith?

DISCUSSION

Probably the most important part of any Alpha is the chance to share thoughts and ideas on the topic, and simply discuss it in a small group. There's no obligation to say anything. And there's nothing you can't say. It's an opportunity to hear from others and contribute your own perspective in an honest, friendly and open environment.

ALPHA WORKS WHEN IT IS:

Real

When people speak about Jesus authentically, unreligiously but unapologetically, and pray in the power of the Holy Spirit, we often see people's lives are changed. It's not always easy or straightforward but it is effective! Alpha is about authenticity; those running Alpha are real with the guests, which in turn creates space for the guests to be real and authentic.

Relational

Alpha is about relationships. Ultimately, Alpha revolves around the small group and the friendships that are formed here. It's about a journey, taken together. Everything we do with Alpha is designed to create a welcoming atmosphere—the food, the arrangement of tables and chairs, the centerpieces, and most importantly, those welcoming guests to Alpha. This all takes time, but over the course of several weeks, when sharing in a common faith journey and in each other's lives from week to week, many groups have created friendships that can last for years beyond Alpha.

Reliant

In Alpha, we are reliant on the Holy Spirit. Alpha doesn't change lives; it is the Holy Spirit working in people who changes lives. We must simply be open to him. We do Alpha in partnership with the Spirit. We are involved in God's amazing work which is why it is so important for us to do everything we can to the best of our ability and trust God for him to act.

Reproducible

When you experience the love of God, the natural response is to tell others. Alpha is a way for anybody to share their faith. Alpha provides an opportunity for anyone to use their gifts to touch the lives of the guests. Oftentimes, after experiencing Alpha, guests want to get involved, to be able to impact the lives of people in a powerful way. The good news is, there are plenty of ways to help with Alpha —as a host or helper, welcoming guests, preparing food, prayer team etc. Ultimately, Alpha should be run in a way that is reproducible. In other words, someone interested in doing something similar should be able to look at your Alpha and know that they too could do this. With the right team, anyone can run Alpha!

TOOLS AVAILABLE

Running an effective Alpha involves planning. We have created a number of tools and resources to help make the process as easy as possible. Use this handbook as well as our online training center called Alpha Builder to get all the support you need. You can access Alpha Builder at run.alphausa. org or run.alphacanada.org.

Within Alpha Builder you can create an Alpha which will provide access to all of the digital resources (videos, promotional materials, etc.) you need to get started. Here you can view and download the Alpha talks that are right for your audience - Alpha Film Series, Alpha with Nicky Gumbel, or the Alpha Youth Series.

There are a total of 15 talks (including those covered on the Alpha weekend).

Alpha explores these questions:
Is There More to Life Than This?
Who Is Jesus?
Why Did Jesus Die?
How Can I Have Faith?
Why and How Do I Pray?
Why and How Do I Read the Bible?
How Does God Guide Us?
Who Is the Holy Spirit?*
What Does the Holy Spirit Do?*
How Can I Be Filled with the Holy
  Spirit?*
How Can I Make the Most of the Rest
  of My Life?*
How Can I Resist Evil?
Why and How Should I Tell Others?
Does God Heal Today?
What About the Church?

*These questions are explored on the Alpha weekend or day.

Each of these talks, as well as the customizable scripts for live talks, are available for free through Alpha Builder. Here you can also access training materials for your team, promotional materials and all of the information you need to make your Alpha a success!

TRAIN

Alpha has created tools and training videos to support you as the Alpha administrator. Additionally, resources are available to help train the rest of your team. These resources will help answer the most common questions about food, teambuilding, atmosphere, prayer and the essentials of a quality Alpha. Also, be sure to check online for any upcoming Run Alpha training events. Run Alpha training provides a practical introduction to what Alpha looks like. It may also provide you with an opportunity to connect with churches who have been running Alpha for years, as well as those who are exploring or just running it for the first time.

Hospitality

Showing up to Alpha for the first time can be extremely intimidating for some guests—especially for someone who wouldn't typically go to church. That's why we suggest creating a welcoming and fun atmosphere. Hospitality helps people feel like they belong.

When we put some effort into creating a welcoming and fun atmosphere, guests are more likely to enjoy themselves, build relationships, engage in the discussion and keep coming back each week! And they will feel comfortable enough to tell their friends about Alpha.

The key to creating a positive atmosphere for your Alpha is to think of it like a casual party. We aim to set the mood as if we're welcoming guests into our home. Here are some ideas from churches who made their Alpha a bit more inviting.

WE HOPE THIS WILL HELP SPARK YOUR CREATIVITY:

Food

Eating a meal or a snack together allows guests to have a space for casual conversations and to get to know each other. Remember to provide a meat-free option and to ask about allergies.

Venue

Run Alpha where people are most likely to show up. Think about who you're trying to reach and where they spend their time. Most Alphas take place in a church, but Alpha has also been run in places like coffee shops, high schools, homes, gyms, pubs, and even bike shops.

Room Decor

The way you set up the room, including things like table setup (centerpieces, place settings),

signage (welcome sign, menu, food labels) and even lights (candles, table and floor lamps) contribute to the overall guest experience. Try to be creative each week because these details make the Alpha experience memorable especially when targeted to the demographic you are trying to reach.

Seating

You want seating that will make conversation easy. Try to steer away from office or classroom set up and aim for small groups of 8-12. Use whatever is available—try small coffee tables instead of big tables, big comfy couches, floor pillows— anything that will help people relax.

Music

Depending on your context and audience, play upbeat music or invite a local artist to play during meal time. Some groups slowly introduce Christian music and worship after the Alpha weekend and some begin with it right away. Whenever you choose to introduce it, it helps to explain why worship is a key element of Christian life.

Temperature

Monitor this throughout the night because if it gets too warm, guests will feel uncomfortable and possibly fall asleep during the Alpha talk. The more people that are in the room, the warmer it will get as the night progresses.

Fun

Laughing together is one of the best ways to build a sense of community and friendship. It can lighten the mood, bridge over awkward dynamics and allow people to relax. Depending on your group's age and context, you can start with a funny, neutral video clip, tell a joke, or do a short icebreaker game.

Food and Alpha

Food helps set the tone and puts people at ease. It's also one of the easiest ways to make people feel welcome. It gives guests the opportunity to come together, share a meal and get to know one another on a deeper level.

THREE WAYS OF ORGANIZING THE MEAL:

Church catering team

Organize a catering team from within your church or organization to provide the food for Alpha every week or on a rotating basis. Keep the budget to a minimum, and invite your guests to make a contribution to the cost of the meal by suggesting a small donation ($5.00). Provide a secure or enclosed box for donations.

The Alpha small group

If you have a small Alpha group, each week one member of the group could provide the food. You might start by asking all the hosts and helpers to contribute, and often after week five, one of the guests will offer to provide food or the dessert. Always keep this optional and not mandatory for the guests.

Professional catering

As your Alpha grows you may need a caterer. The disadvantage is that it often raises the cost of the meal. You can also hold Alpha in a café or restaurant where they provide the food at a reduced price. Also, check with your team to see who they know. Oftentimes team members have connections to restaurant owners or food providers. Many times these groups will donate a meal to Alpha or will offer a discounted rate for food.

MENU PLANNING AND OTHER GENERAL THOUGHTS:

❐ Pinterest is full of great ideas on cooking for a crowd.

❐ Keep meals simple.

❐ Consider your space. If guests aren't at regular dinner tables, opt for meals that can be eaten in a bowl or ones that don't require utensils, etc.

❒ Offer a non-meat and possibly a gluten-free option as well as a meat option the first few weeks until you determine the dietary preferences of your guests.

❒ If cooking for a large group, check with a local butcher who might give you a good price on bulk orders.

❒ Plan your menu ahead of time so you can watch for sales on non-perishable items.

❒ Buffet style is generally the best way to serve the food. Consider providing servers who can portion out the food onto plates so everyone gets at least one helping.

Listening Leaders

Usually after the first Alpha session, guests are assigned to a small group (by age and/or with friends). The ideal size for a small group on Alpha is between 8-12 people, including two or four hosts and helpers. The goal is that the small group would stay together for the duration of Alpha, go on the journey together, and hopefully become friends along the way.

Ideally your groups would sit together, eat together, watch the Alpha talk and then discuss it right where they are. This helps your group connect, and it saves time since there's no transition to another room or space. Your Alpha leader will explain how it will work.

We use the terms "host" and "helper" because on Alpha it's less about being a leader and more about helping facilitate a conversation. We want people to feel welcomed and included. The format is not teacher/student, but rather host/guest. Note: There are two team training videos to help you learn about how to host great small groups,

and tips on praying for others. Take some time to discuss these with your team.

WHAT DO HOSTS AND HELPERS DO?

Simply put, hosts are the ones who facilitate the small group discussion. Helpers are there to help the host and the guests with anything that might make the group experience even better. Helpers mostly stay quiet. They listen and pray silently as the discussion is unfolding. Being a helper on Alpha is actually one of the best ways for people to step into a leadership role for the first time.

FOR THE ALPHA YOUTH SERIES:

Small group discussion is not only after the Alpha talks, but included throughout each episode. There are several pause prompts with questions for you to discuss with your small group. Take about 5-10 minutes and if you want more time to chat, there are additional questions in the discussion guide to go through at the end of the talk.

FROM GOOD TO GREAT

Show guests that they're valuable by being 100% committed and consistent. Attend all the team training sessions, the Alpha weekend and all the small group discussions. Show genuine care for them by remembering their names and asking how their week is going. Remember, Alpha isn't about "information transfer," it's about friendship.

Keep the Conversation Alive

SHARE THESE GUIDELINES WITH YOUR SMALL GROUP

- You don't have to talk if you don't want to, but we'd love to hear everyone's thoughts.
- Any question or comment is welcome (just be brief and respectful).
- Respect each other by listening and allowing different opinions.
- Keep things confidential when you leave this group.

Small Group Discussion

The heart of Alpha is the small group. This is where people can ask questions, talk through issues, build relationships and experience what the Christian life really looks like. Use the discussion questions that are provided in the Alpha Team Guide, but don't feel like you have to get through all of them. The questions are simply suggestions to help you spark key conversations. Be open to questions that guests have on their own. It will take practice to keep the conversation balanced. Watch for people who tend to dominate and engage those who seem disengaged or shy.

FACILITATING DISCUSSION

One thing that can help in forming the small groups is to use the information gathered from the Guest Sign-Up Form (Appendix F) and put all who check "Christian" in the same group. Their small group will probably have more of a discipleship emphasis.

When guests ask a question, ask the rest of the group what they think or feel about it. If you answer all the questions, there will be no discussion and your answer will be viewed as "the final answer." We want to encourage honest conversation.

Occasionally in the first few weeks, a small group host finds a guest in their group who is quick to answer questions during the small group time. If this occurs, privately remind them the purpose of Alpha is first to listen. Other guests will feel shut down if this is left unattended. If addressed the discussion will flow with more freedom.

Conversation Tips

QUESTIONS

- What do you think about the talk?
- How do you feel about the talk?
- Yes, good question! What do the rest of you think?
- Can you explain a bit more, or give an example?
- Are you wondering if...? (clarify, rephrase)
- Has anyone else felt that way too?
- And how does that make you feel?
- Can you share with us how that question came up for you?

AFFIRMATIONS

- Thank you for sharing that.
- I appreciate your honesty. Tell us more.
- Yes, I can relate to that too!
- It's okay to take a minute and think about it. That's what we're here for. No rush.
- It's okay to have different opinions and disagree. Discussion helps us learn other viewpoints.
- I'm glad you're here!
- Very interesting perspective!

Materials

Many of the resources you need to run your Alpha, including the Alpha talks, are available to you for free through Alpha Builder. DVDs of the Alpha talks as well as other accompanying materials are available for purchase from the Alpha Store/Bookstore.

Plan ahead and determine what type of resources you'll be using, and ensure anything you need is available and delivered prior to beginning Alpha.

Location

The good news...you can run Alpha anywhere! Currently, Alpha is running in homes, cafés, churches, pubs, and all sorts of other locations all around the world. It doesn't matter what venue you choose; simply do what you can to make the space welcoming and conducive to good conversation.

Talks

Based on your audience and the abilities of your team, consider which talks are best suited for your Alpha—several options are available on video to suit different styles, audiences, and contexts. Additionally, scripts are available for those interested in presenting live talks.

Training

Choosing the right team is crucial. The people who host and help in the small groups need to be the best people to both welcome new people into the community and guide discussions in a way that allows for real exploration.

WHO'S ON THE TEAM?

The most helpful question to ask when considering someone for the role of host or helper is, "Would I trust my non-Christian best friend with this person?" If the answer is no, then keep looking for the right people.

It is also important to train your team well. Although Alpha has a simple format, there are a few critical things to remember when running an Alpha small group. Even your hosts and helpers who have done Alpha several times can benefit from attending training before you begin your Alpha.

Training
& Teams

Six Key Alpha Team Roles

ALPHA ADMINISTRATOR:

The administrator carries the overall responsibility of running Alpha, leading the team and delegating tasks.

The administrator is:
- well-organized, detail-oriented
- able to communicate well with a volunteer team
- friendly
- one who values prayer
- encouraging and approachable

The administrator is responsible for:
- scheduling and planning the meetings to train the Alpha team
- determining the day and time when Alpha will run
- securing the venue/location for the weekly gathering
- overseeing the small groups or delegating to the small group coordinator (if it is a larger Alpha)
- planning and securing the venue for the Alpha weekend
- leading the weekly team meetings as well as ongoing team coaching
- working with church leadership to understand and promote Alpha
- arranging the proper resources for the team and guests (Alpha Guides, Alpha Team Guides, additional resources)
- customizing Team and Guest Feedback Forms (see Appendix G and H) at the end of each Alpha
- scheduling post-Alpha evaluation meetings to determine if any changes need to made for the next Alpha

SMALL GROUP HOSTS AND HELPERS

The small group hosts and helpers maintain a safe environment for guests to share openly.

Hosts are:
- warm and caring
- good listeners
- friendly
- okay with silence in the group
- able to facilitate the conversation during the small group time
- willing to pray for the small group on a regular basis

Helpers are:
- warm, caring and friendly
- good listeners
- proactive and seek out the quieter guests to befriend them
- happy to allow others to speak first in the small group
- willing to pray quietly while the small group is meeting
- willing to pray for the small group on a regular basis

EMCEE

This is someone who can host your Alpha each week—welcoming guests with a short introduction, guiding people through each part of the evening, and encouraging guests to come back. This is a key role since the Emcee sets the tone for the evening. Think of one or two people who don't mind speaking in front of groups and can make people feel at ease, especially if they don't typically go to church. It generally helps to lean towards a younger person. In some situations, this role is well suited for a pastor.

HOSPITALITY TEAM

This fun, servant-hearted crew of volunteers cooks the meals, takes care of logistics, greets people and provides administrative support.

SET UP/TEAR DOWN CREW:
- assists with set-up of the Alpha space
- sets up tables, chairs, helps create the atmosphere
- ensures that other tools and resources for the team are ready and available
- assists with tear down and clean up after Alpha

TECH SUPPORT:
- ensures the right audio and visual gear are set up and tested so that everything goes smoothly

DECOR TEAM LEADER:
- dreams up creative ways to make the meeting space more welcoming and fun
- probably loves to spend a lot of time on Pinterest

MEAL COORDINATOR:
- secures a team to assist in the meal preparation and clean up*
- plans the menus
- works with the Alpha administrator to plan the budget
- purchases the food
- oversees the preparation and serving of the food
- delegates and manages the cleanup
- understands this team is vital to the success of Alpha

*Some meal teams gather the names of all the hosts, helpers and small group guests in order to pray for them while washing dishes or preparing food.

GREETERS:
If you have a larger Alpha it's a good idea to have a few friendly people available to help with this.

- welcomes guests at the entrance(s)
- assists them to the childcare area (if offered)
- shows them where the food is being served
- introduces them to their small group

ADMIN SUPPORT:
- helps the Alpha administrator to have things run smoothly before, during and after Alpha
- assists with greeting and registering guests
- helps direct guests as to where to go and what to do next

WORSHIP LEADER

Often the people who find singing worship songs the most difficult at the start of Alpha comment that it is the most enjoyable part by the end. Group worship singing is only recommended if your Alpha is over 25 people. Delegate your worship leadership well in advance. Here are some options:

Some Alphas include worship music from week 1, others begin at weeks 3, 4 or 5.

Some Alphas opt to play a secular song the first week or two and then transition to worship.

If you plan to have worship at the Alpha weekend consider introducing one or two worship songs on Alpha evenings beforehand.

If you don't have live music, at some point on Alpha it might be an idea to play a worship CD or music through your mobile device, even in the background, to allow guests to become familiar with the songs.

PRAYER TEAM

This team prays for your Alpha regularly. Be intentional about praying not only for logistics, but for each guest, host and helper weekly. Many prayer teams commit to gathering and praying for Alpha as it is happening each week.

Four Tips for Building Strong Alpha Teams

1. MATCH PEOPLE UP WITH ROLES THEY LOVE DOING

People enjoy volunteering when their gifts are being used. Find the administrative people and invite them to help with planning. Invite those with the gift of serving and hospitality to be Alpha greeters, servers, and registration helpers. Those who love praying can be on the prayer team. There's a place for everyone on the Alpha team!

2. TAKE YOUR WHOLE TEAM THROUGH THE TWO ALPHA TEAM TRAINING SESSIONS: SMALL GROUPS AND PRAYER & THE WEEKEND

Even if some of your volunteers have done the training before, we suggest that everyone attends the training sessions. It's a great refresher and it ensures that everyone is on the same page and feels like part of the team. The training videos are available for download in Alpha Builder and on the Alpha DVDs.

Note: You can do two sessions in one training day or split them up and watch the video on Prayer & The Weekend closer to your Alpha weekend. Have fun when you get your team together — host a meal or provide snacks, do an icebreaker, share some laughs, provide time for Q&A.

3. MEET WITH YOUR TEAM EACH WEEK DURING ALPHA

Usually teams meet together about 30 minutes before Alpha begins. It's a time to share key info or tips for that session, answer any questions and then pray together.

4. GET FEEDBACK

Some groups debrief each week if time allows, but we definitely encourage you to get together with your team after Alpha has ended. Maybe have a meal with them, thank them for their commitment, time and effort, and talk about what went well and what could be improved.

NEXT STEPS

Take a moment and think of some people who might be excited to be part of your Alpha team and write down their names. Pray about what role they can do. Next open up your calendar and schedule a time for team training if you haven't already.

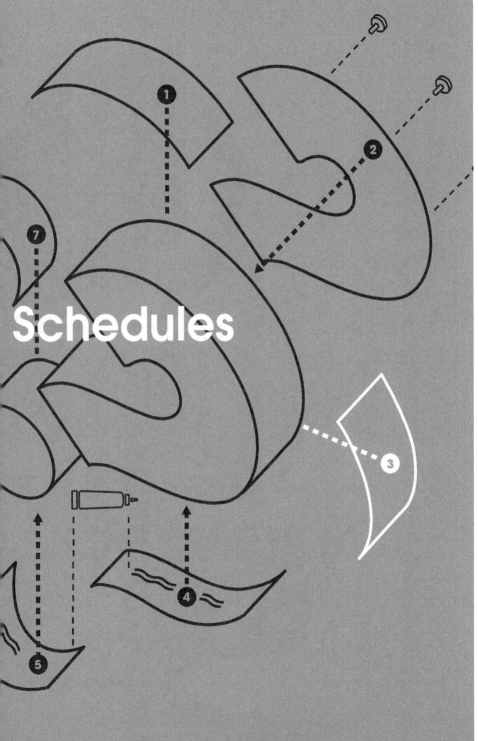

Schedules

Scheduling Your Alpha

WHEN SHOULD WE RUN ALPHA?

It is helpful to think through a few things when deciding when and where to run your Alpha. First understand your audience - who are you hoping to draw to Alpha? What times, days and locations work well for this group? Often church calendars book up months in advance, so it may be wise to schedule two or three Alphas a year. Alpha gains momentum as guests talk about their experience and invite friends to try the next one.

DATE

The first thing to do is to plan your dates. Try to avoid booking your Alpha over any holidays or events that might cause long gaps between sessions or that may cause guests to be unable to attend. For example, running Alpha over Christmas or during school breaks might mean some of your guests will not be able to attend during certain weeks. Think of dates when you can schedule team training (we recommend two training sessions) as well as a launch party and when your Alpha weekend will occur.

TIME

A typical Alpha runs in the evening, but Alpha can be held at any time of day. Think through what time works best for the people you are trying to invite. For example, if you are running Alpha with college students, an early morning breakfast might not be the best option. Whatever time you choose, make sure that you have enough time for food, a talk and a discussion.

SAMPLE ALPHA SESSION AND SCHEDULE

Typically Alpha is 11 weeks, including a weekend or day away.
Customize these schedules as needed for your group.

Alpha Film Series and Alpha with Nicky Gumbel Schedule

Team Training Small Groups (1–2 weeks before the start of Alpha)

Week 1   Is There More to Life Than This? *Launch party
Week 2   Who Is Jesus?
Week 3   Why Did Jesus Die?
Week 4   How Can I Have Faith?
Week 5   Why and How Do I Pray?
Week 6   Why and How Do I Read the Bible?
Week 7   How Does God Guide Us?

Team Training Prayer & The Weekend (prior to the Alpha weekend)

Alpha Weekend

Introduction to the Weekend
Who is the Holy Spirit?
What Does the Holy Spirit Do?
How Can I Be Filled with the Holy Spirit?
How Can I Make the Most of the Rest of My Life?

Week 8   How Can I Resist Evil?
Week 9   Why and How Should I Tell Others?
Week 10   Does God Heal Today?
Week 11   What About the Church?

*A launch party can kick off the start of your Alpha. This may include a nicer
meal, real silverware, lively background music and small groups where you focus
on the icebreaker questions in the Alpha Team Guide and use the Guest Sign-
Up Form found in Appendix F.

WEEKLY SESSIONS

Use this timeline as a starting point for your Alpha and adjust as
needed to fit your setting.

TEAM PREPARATION

1 hr before	Set up and food preparation
30 min before	Alpha team meeting and prayer

ALPHA BEGINS

10 min	Greet guests and encourage people to begin eating
45 min	Dinner and casual conversation
10 min	Worship music (optional)
30 min	Alpha talk
45 min	Small group discussion

ALPHA ENDS

15 min	Debrief with Alpha team

ALPHA PLANNING CHECKLIST

1-3 Months in Advance

❐ Go to Alpha Builder and create your Alpha. You can also choose to publish your Alpha on the website which will help guests search for and find an Alpha in their area.

❐ Watch the leader training videos and preview all of the resources found online.

❐ Edit the specific dates of your Alpha in Alpha Builder (including your team training meetings, weekly sessions, the Alpha weekend or day, holidays, etc.).

❐ Prayerfully select your Alpha team members. (Full descriptions of team roles can be found in the section on Six Key Alpha Team Roles.)

❐ Consider attending a local Run Alpha training with your team. See the events tab for training opportunities in your area at alphausa.org or connect with a Regional Director at alphacanada.org/team.

❐ Develop a budget and a system of accounting for all income and expenses including the following:

- Launch party/intro night
- Weekly meals
- Atmosphere and decor
- Promotional materials
- Alpha weekend/day

Make sure you have someone overseeing the following areas:
- Food prep for each week
- Fundraising (if necessary)
- Prayer

☐ Check on insurance coverage and liability. Make arrangements to cover all aspects as needed.

☐ Check out potential Alpha weekend facilities and book one as soon as possible.

☐ Send a letter (either via email or post) from the pastor to all who are new to the church inviting them to Alpha (or new since the last time Alpha was offered).

1-2 Months in Advance

☐ Go through Alpha Builder and finish up any parts you haven't completed, such as watch the leader training videos, confirm the weekly schedule, add your team members, download the videos, etc.

☐ Plan and prepare food arrangements. Schedule a meeting with the kitchen team members.

☐ Finalize the budget for all aspects of Alpha including weekly meals, the weekend/day, Alpha resources, and other incidentals.

☐ Select an appropriate playlist or specific music for each weekly session. Check on what kind of legal permission you need to print and display the lyrics.

☐ Organize and plan aspects of your Alpha weekend or day. See the Planning an Effective Alpha Weekend Away.

☐ Six weeks out from the start of Alpha, send an email to all past Alpha participants letting them know when Alpha is starting again and encourage them to pray about who to invite.

☐ Five or six weeks from the start of Alpha, use the online promo resources to research, plan and customize promotional material within Alpha Builder. If in the US, you can use the print shop for banners, postcards and invitations at alpharesources.org.

☐ Five weeks out, begin to advertise Alpha in the bulletin or as a PPT slide, and mention it in the weekly announcements.

☐ Four weeks out and every week until Alpha begins, either show a short Alpha teaser, or a video or live testimony at Sunday worship.

☐ Encourage small group hosts and helpers to begin praying for their (potential) group members.

2 Weeks in Advance

☐ Get your Alpha team together to watch the team training videos, talk about team roles, the timeline, and have fun.

☐ Meet with your decor team and brainstorm ways to create a welcoming atmosphere. Think about lighting, seating, table centerpieces, etc.

☐ Finalize food arrangements depending on the number of guests you expect.

☐ Continue to advertise Alpha in the bulletin or as a PPT slide and mention it in the weekly announcements.

☐ Continue to show a short Alpha teaser, or a video or live testimony at Sunday worship.

Weekly Alpha Sessions

☐ Arrange for the Alpha team to arrive early for set up, create a welcoming atmosphere, and prepare for the session.

☐ Double check that all audio-visual equipment is in place before guests arrive. Set up the TV or projector screen, projector or computer, microphone and speakers as needed. (Download the videos in advance to avoid potential streaming issues.)

☐ Make sure there are enough Bibles and Alpha Guides. (optional).

☐ Each week, meet with your whole Alpha team for prayer and updates before everyone goes to their places.

☐ Have a team of people praying while small groups are meeting.

☐ On week two or three, place a donation box in an area that is secure but visible (optional).

☐ Promote dates for the Alpha weekend early. Build it up as a fun getaway.

☐ Debrief with your Alpha team after guests go home.

☐ Celebrate the small wins, talk about what to improve and encourage each other.

Weeks Leading up to the Alpha Weekend

☐ Finalize the number of people who will be attending the Alpha weekend.

❒ Oversee the purchase and preparation of food provided for the Alpha weekend.

❒ Develop the schedule (including leisure time) and communicate this to your team and guests. Determine how/when music will be included.

❒ Select a team to oversee worship music and prayer ministry.

❒ Hand out copies of your weekend/day schedule, map of the facility, waiver form for minors, and list of things to bring (as needed).

One Week Before the Alpha Weekend

❒ Meet with your team to watch the team training video called Prayer & The Weekend and talk about what the weekend will look like for your group.

❒ Arrive early for set-up and to create a fun and friendly atmosphere.

❒ Double check that all audio-visual equipment is in place before guests arrive.

Week After Alpha Ends

❒ Meet with your Alpha team to go over Alpha Guest and Team Feedback Forms to evaluate and improve aspects of your Alpha and to share stories.

❒ Send a thank you email or card to all team members who have helped throughout Alpha (don't forget the prayer team!).

Alpha
Weekend

Plan Your Alpha Weekend

The Alpha weekend is all about getting away from the busyness of everyday life so people can connect with each other and connect with God. It's the part of Alpha that many people say was the turning point in their Alpha experience. We consistently see hearts more open to Jesus and lives changed. And that's why we do it.

The weekend or day away is a significant part of the Alpha experience and quite often proves to be the part which guests find most transformative. It's worth putting effort into planning. One way to make the process easier is to pair up with another Alpha in your city and run a weekend together.

The Alpha weekend provides guests an opportunity to get to know each other. If possible, select a time and place different from where you usually meet. Create an experience for guests that allows them to relax and get away from daily concerns and stresses. The weekend should include an element of fun and "down time" where guests can choose how they'd like to spend their time. It is important to build this in, as the material covered on the weekend away impacts each guest differently. Many will welcome an opportunity to step away and relax between sessions.

The typical Alpha weekend runs from Friday night to Sunday morning. This creates unhurried time and space to watch all the talks about the Holy Spirit, for waiting on God and praying together, and for people to relax and have fun.

For some groups, getting away for a whole weekend is not possible. Sometimes people can only do the Friday night and all day Saturday, or even just one full day. It does take some planning but it's worth it!

WHY DO THE ALPHA WEEKEND?

• It gives guests the space, time, and atmosphere needed to thoroughly process and reflect on what they are learning.

• It helps guests, hosts and helpers get to know each other better and form lasting relationships. Three or four of the teachings are given during the weekend (25% of the Alpha material).

• It provides an opportunity for guests to ask to be prayed for and filled with the Holy Spirit.

• It's a special time to let God bless and encourage guests and leaders.

SAMPLE ALPHA WEEKEND 3 DAY SCHEDULE

FRIDAY

6:00 pm	Arrive
7:00 pm	Dinner or snacks
8:00 pm	Introduction / icebreaker game
9:00 pm	Show Intro to the Alpha weekend video

SATURDAY

8:30 am	Breakfast
9:00 am	Leaders' meeting
9:30 am	Weekend Talk #1: Who Is the Holy Spirit?
10:00 am	Refreshments and snacks
10:30 am	Weekend Talk #2: What Does the Holy Spirit Do?
11:00 am	Small group discussion
12:00 pm	Lunch
2:00 pm	Free time (activities can be organized)
4:00 pm	Snacks, coffee and tea
5:00 pm	Worship & Weekend Talk #3: How Can I Be Filled with the Holy Spirit?
5:30 pm	Prayer ministry time
6:30 pm	Dinner
8:00 pm	Free time

SUNDAY

9:00 am	Breakfast
9:30 am	Leaders' meeting
10:00 am	Small group discussion
11:00 am	Weekend Talk #4: How Can I Make the Most of My Life?
11:30 am	Prayer ministry time
12:00 pm	Lunch and depart

*Your schedule may change depending on your Alpha material and number of talks you have on the weekend.

**If your weekend is only 2 days, adjust the Intro to the weekend video to be at the start of the day.

SAMPLE ALPHA WEEKEND 1 DAY SCHEDULE

SATURDAY

9:15 am	Arrive, registration, and coffee
9:45 am	Worship music
9:30 am	Weekend Talks #1: Who Is the Holy Spirit and #2: What Does He Do?
10:30 am	Refreshments and small groups
11:15 am	Worship Music
11:30 am	Weekend Talk #3: How Can I Be Filled with the Holy Spirit?
12:00 pm	Prayer ministry time
1:00 pm	Lunch and free time (walks, rest)
2:00 pm	Refreshments
2:15 pm	Worship Music
2:30 pm	Weekend Talk #4: How Can I Make the Most of the Rest of My Life?
3:00 pm	Optional small group time or finish

Tip #1

Go to a house, cabin, retreat center nearby — just somewhere different from the usual meeting space.

Tip #2

Watch the Prayer & The Weekend training video with your whole team before the Alpha weekend so they feel prepared.

Tip #3

Calling it the Alpha weekend or day away is more inviting than referring to it as the Holy Spirit weekend. In your promotional resources, highlight the relational connections!

Tip #4

Make your Alpha weekend or day away FUN! This is a great chance to solidify the relationships that are developing on Alpha.

PLANNING AN EFFECTIVE WEEKEND AWAY

1-3 months ahead:

Item:	Contact Person:	Notes:	Done:
Decide how long the retreat will be (weekend, 1, 2 or 3 days).			
Pick a date (or dates) for the retreat.			
Assign planning duties: logistics, sports, child care, transportation, etc.			
Draft a tentative schedule.			
Reserve a retreat site.			
If retreat site does not include food, reserve caterer.			
Draft tentative budget.			
Meet with team to discuss duties and pray.			

PLANNING AN EFFECTIVE WEEKEND AWAY

1-3 months ahead:

Item:	Contact Person:	Notes:	Done:
Finalize the retreat schedule.			
Organize transportation arrangements if necessary.			
Visit the retreat site if you haven't been there before.			
Prepare retreat brochure including map, cost, what to bring, waiver form (if needed), allergies, special diets, medical conditions.			
Meet with your team to discuss duties and pray.			
Follow up with your team to discuss tasks assigned.			

PLANNING AN EFFECTIVE WEEKEND AWAY

1 months ahead:

Item:	Contact Person:	Notes:	Done:
Order Alpha resources to sell/give at retreat (e.g. *Why Jesus?* booklets, *Searching Issues* books)			
Meet with your team to discuss duties and pray.			
Follow up with your team to discuss tasks assigned.			

PLANNING AN EFFECTIVE WEEKEND AWAY

2-3 weeks ahead:

Item:	Contact Person:	Notes:	Done:
Distribute retreat brochure and waiver form (if needed) to guests.			
Confirm with the retreat site re details.			
Confirm food/catering arrangements.			
Gather equipment/supplies into one area (see sample list below).			
Confirm audio-visual equipment is taken care of.			
Meet with your team to discuss duties and pray.			
Plan to take a special offering Sunday morning to cover the expenses of those unable to pay full amount for retreat.			

PLANNING AN EFFECTIVE WEEKEND AWAY

1 week ahead:

Item:	Contact Person:	Notes:	Done:
Small group hosts collect registration fees or deposit.			
Prepare photocopying/printing of any handouts.			
Draft up room assignments.			
Inform caterer about dietary restrictions and allergies.			
Review the schedule one final time, make any changes.			
Create door signs with names.			

PLANNING AN EFFECTIVE WEEKEND AWAY

Item:	Contact Person:	Notes:	Done:
Remind guests to bring their Alpha Guest Guides, Bibles, sports equipment, games etc.			
Print copies of the retreat map and room assignments to post up at main entrance.			
Prepare thank you cards and final checks if applicable.			
Meet with your team to watch the team training video called Prayer & The Weekend. Discuss duties, Pray together.			

PLANNING AN EFFECTIVE WEEKEND AWAY

During Retreat:

Item:	Contact Person:	Notes:	Done:
Enjoy!			
Post up the retreat map, schedule and room assignments at main entrance.			
Meet with team leaders for prayer and any questions.			
Reserve facilities for next retreat (if applicable).			
Ensure the retreat site is left clean and orderly.			

PLANNING AN EFFECTIVE WEEKEND AWAY

Post Retreat:

Item:	Contact Person:	Notes:	Done:
Review the retreat budget (make notes for next retreat).			
Make note of what worked and didn't work for next time.			
Arrange for testimonies at the next Alpha session and/or Sunday service.			

THINGS TO CONSIDER FOR THE RETREAT:

- ❐ Alpha resources including *Why Jesus?* booklets
- ❐ Bibles, extra
- ❐ Carpooling information
- ❐ Contact list with cell numbers
- ❐ Calculator
- ❐ Communion supplies (if applicable)
- ❐ First aid kit
- ❐ Flipchart paper
- ❐ Kleenex
- ❐ Markers
- ❐ Maps
- ❐ Name tags
- ❐ New Christian resources
- ❐ Pens and pencils
- ❐ PowerPoint projector (if needed)
- ❐ Prizes for games (if needed)
- ❐ Pulpit stand/lectern
- ❐ Room assignment list
- ❐ Schedule, copies
- ❐ Songbooks or songsheets (if needed)
- ❐ Sports equipment
- ❐ Thank you cards

More Guests

Promoting Your Alpha and Inviting Others

Once you've created your Alpha within Alpha Builder, make sure that you promote it. This allows people to find you on the website. We often hear of people who attend Alpha just from searching for it in their area on our website. It's great if they can find you and come along. To access Alpha Builder go to run.alphausa.org or run.alphacanada.org.

Each year Alpha provides a range of promotional materials which can be found online. There are posters, postcards, banners and other print materials. We also have a range of images and videos to use with social media. These invitational materials are a visible way of letting your wider community know about Alpha, but it's important to note, the main way people come to Alpha is through a personal invitation. Make sure that your church or organization gets on board and that everyone invites their friends along. Pray for creativity, and think through how you are going to encourage people to invite their friends and how you will advertise your Alpha to the local community.

> **The best invitation is from a friend, without pressure.**

Sharing the Experience

When Alpha guests have a positive experience, they tell their friends about it, and invite them to the next Alpha. In fact 86% of guests come to Alpha because of a personal invitation. Things like print and digital advertising and Facebook invitations can help, but advertising at its best simply raises awareness and helps set up a personal invitation. The best thing you can do is to inspire and equip your team of volunteers and Alpha guests to invite others. Here are some ways to make inviting others easier:

1. SHARE STORIES

Have one or two people who have just experienced Alpha for themselves tell their story to your church. If you haven't done Alpha before, use one of the Alpha video stories from our blog —alphausa.org/blog or alphacanada.org/blog. Stories are the best way to share the heart of what Alpha is all about.

2. PROVIDE PROMOTIONAL TOOLS

We have a variety of print and digital assets available for free that you can customize with your Alpha details. Get them into the hands of your team and Alpha guests so they have something to give to their friends as an extension of their invitation.

3. ENCOURAGE YOUR TEAM TO INVITE

It takes a bit of courage and risk to share something that's important to you, but it's worth the effort. Alpha could be an experience that someone else is looking for.

4. PRAY

Pray together as a team that God would bring to mind the people he wants you to invite and will give you the opportunities and the courage you need to extend those invitations.

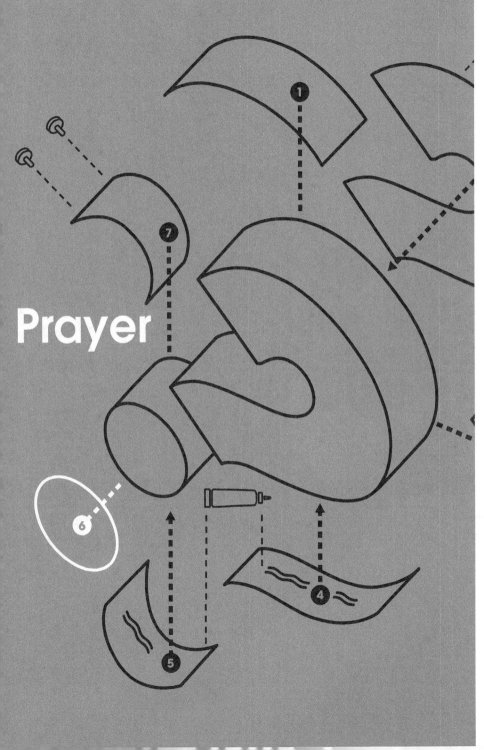

Prayer

Pray

Prayer is essential on Alpha. In fact, this is the most important thing you can do for your Alpha!

Here are a few suggestions:

1. GET YOUR WHOLE CHURCH PRAYING.

Spend time praying for Alpha in your church services, small groups and prayer meetings. Even if your Alpha will take place on a college campus, in your local coffee shop or somewhere else outside of the church, get everyone you can to pray. Not only does this make a difference, but it also helps keep Alpha in the minds of the church and reminds them to invite their friends to the next one.

2. GET PEOPLE TO PRAY TOGETHER BEFORE EACH SESSION OF ALPHA.

During the team meeting at the start of each Alpha session, take time to pray with the Alpha hosts, helpers and team. Pray for one another, the talk, and the guests.

3. GET HOSTS AND HELPERS PRAYING FOR EACH GUEST.

Encourage hosts and helpers to pray for every guest in their group, everyday, by name throughout Alpha.

4. GET THE GUESTS PRAYING WHEN THEY ARE READY.

It's exciting when members of your group pray aloud for the first time, offer to pray for one another or report on answered prayers from the week before. When the group is ready, normally on the week when we talk about prayer, we model a short simple prayer and give others the chance to pray if they want to. Some of those first simple prayers are the best.

Prayer on Alpha

One of the foundational values of running Alpha is to rely on God, and prayer is the greatest expression of that value. So take a moment to consider how you will approach each of these different opportunities for prayer. Pray that guests will connect with God and experience his love in a life-changing way.

Prayer is an essential part of the Alpha guest experience and it's introduced gradually in these four ways.

1. PRAYER DURING THE FIRST FEW SESSIONS

Depending on what Alpha series you are watching, there may be a short prayer led by one of the presenters at the end of the talk. This is intended to give guests a chance to pray along silently if they want to.

2. SESSION 5 IS ALL ABOUT PRAYER

Small groups are encouraged to discuss the topic and then try praying together at the end. Group hosts might simply say a short prayer or give guests an opportunity to pray out loud. In the following weeks hosts can choose to end all small group sessions with prayer. Note: On Alpha we recommend that you do NOT pray before meals or during small group time until Week 5. This allows the topic of prayer to be introduced thoughtfully and discussed thoroughly in small groups.

3. PRAYING FOR OTHERS ON THE ALPHA WEEKEND/DAY AWAY

The Alpha weekend is usually scheduled about halfway through your Alpha. It's a chance to get away from the busyness of our lives, where people can take time to relax, think, have fun together, learn more about God, and if they're willing, to experience prayer ministry. The Alpha talks on the weekend introduce the third person of the Trinity—the Holy Spirit—explaining who the Spirit is and what He does and how the Spirit helps us live in a relationship with Jesus. After the last session, there's time for guests to pray and be prayed for by a host or helper. We want to give them an opportunity to experience God's love through the Holy Spirit. There are leader training videos in Alpha Builder about prayer to help explain this more.

4. PRAYER AND HEALING

After the Alpha talk about healing, we encourage small groups to discuss the topic and take a step of faith—pray for healing! It's often in those prayer times that God surprises us by what he does in people's hearts and in their bodies. Praying for others can be a bit nerve-wracking but if we have even mustard-seed faith, God will show up (Matthew 17:20). God loves to reveal himself to those who sincerely seek him (Hebrews 11:6).

Praying for Others

The word "ministry", simply put, means service. So when we talk about prayer ministry, we are talking about serving people through prayer. If you plan to have someone else lead this time, be sure to coach them through it and have them watch the team training video on Prayer & The Weekend.

After the talk about being filled with the Holy Spirit, groups are encouraged to wait on God, and ask him to fill them with his Holy Spirit. Since all groups and contexts are unique, there isn't a perfect formula or exact model to do this, but here are three helpful tips:

INVITE AND WAIT

Start with a prayer for everyone in the room. A simple prayer you could pray is, "Come, Holy Spirit, and fill our hearts" or something similar. Then just wait on God - this can be the hard part. Wait for minutes, not just a few seconds. It's amazing how long a minute of silence actually feels – and as you're waiting, encourage guests to be open to what God might want to do and to be patient.

Note: Some groups want to have music playing in the background during prayer time, others prefer to have silence. The main thing is that people would be able to focus on God and not get distracted. You might want to encourage people to stand in silence and hold their hands out as if they're about to receive a gift.

HOST AND HELPERS PRAY

After some time of waiting on God the leader can say, "Now, would the hosts and helpers like to begin to pray for the guests?" And then they can begin to pray for them as appropriate, whether it's for the person to encounter Jesus for the first time, or to be filled with the Spirit, or to receive a new spiritual gift.

INVITE THEM INTO A RELATIONSHIP WITH JESUS

We usually give people an opportunity to pray a prayer of repentance and faith if they want to begin or renew a relationship with Jesus. A sample prayer can be found in the *Why Jesus?* booklet. Then we pray, "Come, Holy Spirit." And we wait for what the Holy Spirit wants to do, and it can be different each time.

Prayer time can take anywhere from 15 minutes to over an hour. After a while, it's great to have someone lead in songs of worship. This time of prayer ministry needs intentional leadership. It takes a bit of preparation, but it is amazing to see all the things God will do. All of this is shaped by a confidence in God and his desire to pour his love into our hearts through the Holy Spirit.

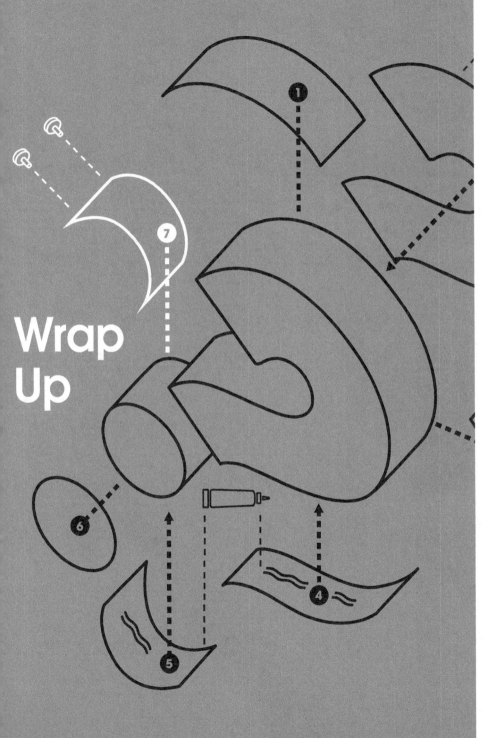

Wrap
Up

After Alpha

As Alpha concludes, guests often ask what is available after Alpha. For many people, the relationships formed within the small groups are strong and they want to continue the connection beyond Alpha. Below are some suggestions and ideas on how to keep your guests engaged.

STAY CONNECTED

Plan a reunion and encourage guests to exchange contact information. Plan a time to get together and connect — perhaps a leisurely brunch or lunch on a weekend.

SEE YOU SUNDAY

Invite your small group to meet at an upcoming Sunday service, so you can all attend church together. This makes it less intimidating if the guests are not regular church attenders.

HELP ON A FUTURE ALPHA

Invite the appropriate guests to help on a future Alpha. Getting guests involved is a sustainable way to build your Alpha team. Former guests are often very enthusiastic about their Alpha experience and can be a great asset to your team. Consider the guests' individual gifts and help them identify a way that they can be involved. Encourage them to think of people they know who might be interested in participating in your next Alpha. If a guest missed several sessions of Alpha, they may want to return again as a guest.

SMALL GROUP

If guests are interested in exploring more of the Christian faith, help them to get connected in a small group at your church. If many in the group feel this way, consider encouraging them to become their own small group.

ALSO FROM ALPHA:

BIBLE IN ONE YEAR

The Bible in One Year is a free Bible reading app with a daily commentary by Nicky and Pippa Gumbel. Since its development in 2009, the app has had over a million unique downloads and subscriptions in 194 countries — many of these readers being Alpha guests.

Download for free on the App Store and Google Play.

THE MARRIAGE COURSES

The Marriage Course and The Marriage Preparation Course act as a bridge between the church and local community by recognizing the need to go beyond the social, as well as physical, walls of the church to help couples with their relationships.

In the USA, visit alphausa.org/the-marriage-courses or in Canada, visit themarriagecourses.ca for more information.

Final Thoughts

While Alpha can be incredibly exciting, it can also be incredibly challenging! It is amazing to see people come alive in their faith, grow in their relationship with God and to watch the impact this has on their families or friends' lives. It is challenging when people are invited and do not come, or if they come one night then don't return. It can be heartbreaking for sure, but our job is to invite! It is the Holy Spirit who reveals the love of Jesus and draws people to the Father.

Bear in mind there is attrition on Alpha. On average you can expect that about 30% of the guests who start Alpha will not finish the eleven weeks. It is normal that only 50% of your guests will attend your weekend or day away. Celebrate if more than 50% attend!

And finally, on average, you will need to run Alpha seven times until you work out how Alpha fits your environment. Alpha is like a snowball. If you offer Alpha two or three times a year, there is a natural synergy that occurs. It also takes about this long for the percentage of non-churchgoing guests to exceed the percentage of churchgoing guests. Don't be discouraged if your Alpha participant numbers are lower than when you started, because the number to watch is how many guests are attending who are not regular church attenders.

Over time, we are confident that running Alpha will spark an even greater culture of hospitality and invitation, empowerment of new leaders, and an expectation that God is going to do something new.

We thank God for you and we are praying for you!

Connect with Alpha

We welcome any opportunity to speak with you. Whether it's hearing your vision or simply assisting you with a question, our team is waiting to talk with you.

Let's connect

alphausa.org/contact
800.362.5742

alphacanada.org/connect
800.743.0899

caribbean.alpha.org/contact
868.671.0133

Tell us your story

Has your life been changed on Alpha? We would love to hear how God worked in your life. It might be just what someone considering attending Alpha needs to hear to take that next step.

Share your story:
USA: #MyAlphaStory

Canada: alphacanada.org/stories

Go deeper in the Word

Start your day with the Bible in One Year, a free Bible reading app with commentary by Nicky and Pippa Gumbel. Receive a daily email or audio commentary coordinated with the Bible in One Year reading plan.

alpha.org/bioy

Join our online communities

Looking for like-minded people who are talking about their recent experience on Alpha? Join the conversation on social media.

Find us on Facebook.

Twitter - @alphausa; @alphacanada; @alphalatam

Instagram - @alphausa | #RunAlpha

Appendices

Appendix A

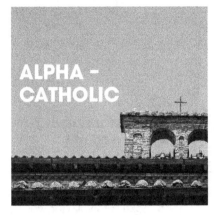

ALPHA -
CATHOLIC

Thanks for running Alpha - Catholic!

We're so excited that God has called you to serve in this capacity and we want to make sure you and your team are equipped and confident to lead.

If you are new to Alpha, here are 5 key benefits of running it in your community:

1. Alpha shares the kerygma ("basic Gospel message") and contributes to parish renewal.

....

2. Alpha enables lay people to exercise their call to be missionary disciples.

....

3. Alpha is a proven form of community evangelization.

....

4. Alpha develops Catholic leaders.

....

5. Alpha works great in conjunction with programs of sacramental preparation.

....

We hope that you find the resources online to be both helpful and convenient. If you have any questions at all, please don't hesitate to contact us: alphausa.org/catholics or alphacanada.org/catholics.

"Alpha brings people closer and helps them to find that power which unites. The Alpha experience is not only a means through which one finds true life, but also a way to share the good news of the Living Christ."

- Cardinal Marc Ouellet

Appendix B

ALPHA - YOUTH

Thanks for running Alpha - Youth!

We're so excited that God has called you to serve in this capacity and we want to make sure you and your team are equipped and confident to lead.

Although every group and context can be different, there are some components to Alpha that make it a success. Here are 5 important key factors to consider:

1. Involve students in leadership and training (for buy in and ownership).

2. Alpha works best when students invite their friends. It's not a Sunday school curriculum. It's an evangelistic tool with a discipleship element and not solely for teens that attend church regularly.

3. Include the essential elements of Alpha such as the team training and the Alpha weekend.

4. Alpha is not a one-time thing. Think about the next time you can run it and encourage your team/guests to think about who to invite.

5. Lots of help is available to help you run a great Alpha. Utilize this network of support!

Visit alphausa.org/youth or alphacanada.org/youth for more information. There are also a number of training videos, Toolbox documents and other helpful resources available in Alpha Builder to help you run a great Alpha.

Also visit alphausa.org/events or alphacanada.org/team to see what events are happening near you.

Got questions? Email youth@alphausa.org or youth@alphacanada.org

Appendix C

ALPHA - PRISON

Thanks for running Alpha - Prison

We're so excited that God has called you to serve in this capacity and we want to make sure you and your team are equipped and confident to lead.

Although every correctional facility and institution is different and some contexts will vary more than others, there are some components to Alpha that make it a success. Here are 5 important key factors to consider when running Alpha in prisons:

1. Before starting, determine all the resources that you will need, including the commitment of leaders and volunteers.

....

2. Select and train your team appropriately and wisely.

....

3. Be extremely familiar with the "Do's and Don'ts" inside the prison concerning your conduct.

....

4. Liaise with your local Alpha – Prisons Coach, Prison Associate and/or Prison National Director so they can support and serve you. They are there to help you.

....

5. Remember that you are there to serve the prison, staff and guests attending Alpha.

....

There are also a number of training videos, Toolbox documents and other helpful resources available in Alpha Builder to help you run a great Alpha.

Visit alphausa.org/events or alphacanada.org/team to see what events are happening near you.

Appendix D

ALPHA
TOOLBOX

ALPHA –
WORKPLACE

Thanks for running Alpha – Workplace!

We're so excited that God has called you to serve in this capacity and we want to make sure you and your team are equipped and confident to lead.

Although every group can be different, there are some components to Alpha in this context that make it a success. Here are 5 important factors to consider:

1. **Get permission to run Alpha at your place of work.** Ensure that you communicate to those in charge that Alpha is open to everyone at your place of work, regardless of their background. Let them know they don't have to endorse Alpha, rather you'd like permission to use the facilities and promote it. If you work in a government office, please ensure that you know the laws relating to a faith-based group meeting on the premises.

2. **Run Alpha in one hour.** Depending on your workplace culture, you can run Alpha during a lunchtime or right after work. Do a short introduction, then show the 30-minute Alpha Film Series videos or present live talks while guests eat lunch or have snacks, and have small group discussion right after. Be considerate of workplace rules and end on time.

3. **Be aware of workplace roles**. Although we don't label guests outwardly, there are still cultural norms. Guests may feel more comfortable discussing life issues if they are with familiar colleagues on the same professional level. Use your best judgment in order to create a good environment for discussion.

4. **Invite people personally.** Although a poster in the cafeteria or a group email invitation can provide lots of information, it's really the one-to-one invitation that convinces people that Alpha is a safe place to talk about life's big questions. Encourage your Alpha team to invite someone in person.

5. **Do the Alpha weekend.** The temptation is to ignore this element of Alpha but this is a key ingredient to one's faith journey as well as building strong relationships with others. Take time to go away somewhere special as a group and allow the Holy Spirit to work in their hearts. This is also a time for guests to be prayed for and experience God in a fresh new way. Often guests say that the Alpha weekend was the best part of Alpha.

There are also a number of training videos, Toolbox documents and other helpful resources available in Alpha Builder to help you run a great Alpha.

Visit alphausa.org/events or alphacanada.org/team to see what events are happening near you.

Appendix E

ALPHA
TOOLBOX

ALPHA - SENIORS

Thanks for running Alpha - Seniors!

We're so excited that God has called you to serve in this capacity and we want to make sure you and your team are equipped and confident to lead.

Although every group can be different, there are some components to Alpha in this context that make it a success. Here are 5 important factors to consider:

1. **Be creative with the structure of your Alpha.** Some guests may have shorter attention spans while others find it difficult to sit for long periods of time. One suggestion is to break the talks into two segments, pausing for discussion halfway through.

2. **Host Alpha where it is easily accessible.** Since many seniors have physical limitations, it is essential to work within the capabilities of your guests. Make sure there are parking stalls reserved for those with disabilities, as well as wheelchair ramps, and helpers to greet guests at the door.

3. **Provide appropriate audio-visual aids.** If possible, use the Alpha talks with subtitles and turn the volume up a little since guests may have difficulty with hearing. Pick a room that has good acoustics and few distractions. Provide guests with the *Why Jesus?* booklet available in larger print.

4. **Be sensitive.** Guests may have faced or be facing difficult situations such as financial loss, bereavement, regret or loneliness. Some may have physical disabilities and for some death will be a real and presenting issue. Others may feel neglected or forgotten by their family and friends. Connect guests with appropriate pastoral care and/or resources.

5. **Run Alpha in the daytime.** Hosting activities in the mornings or early afternoons often work well for seniors. This helps keep seniors safe so they don't have to drive or walk home in the dark. If you're running Alpha in a senior center or care facility, check with the staff first and work around their existing programs.

There are also a number of training videos, Toolbox documents and other helpful resources available in Alpha Builder to help you run a great Alpha.

Visit alphausa.org/events or alphacanada.org/team to see what events are happening near you.

Appendix F

Alpha

Name: _____   ☐ Male   ☐ Female

Age Group:

Under 20 ☐   20-29 ☐   30-39 ☐   40-49 ☐   50-59 ☐   60+ ☐

Would you like to join us for Alpha next week?

☐ Yes I will be there!*   ☐ Not sure yet   ☐ No sorry, I will not be attending

*If yes, please fill in emails and/or phone#: _____

Spiritually speaking, I identify most with:

☐ Searching ☐ Undecided ☐ Skeptical ☐ Spiritual, but no religious affiliation ☐ Christian ☐ Other

Group Preferences:

Please put me in the same group as: _____

Dietary Needs:

Do you have dietary needs?   No ☐   Yes ☐

Please list any food allergies: _____

Appendix G

Guest Feedback Form

Name: (optional) _____   Small Group Host: _____

1. How did you hear about Alpha?

□ Friend/Relative/Colleague   □ Church/Bulletin

□ Facebook/Twitter/Online   □ Poster

□ Outdoor Promo/Banner   □ Other: _____

2. Why did you decide to come to Alpha? (Check all that apply)

□ Someone invited me   □ I was looking for meaning and purpose in life

□ I was curious and it looked interesting   □ Free food

□ I had questions and wanted to find out more

□ Other: _____

3. Did you attend church before taking Alpha?

□ Yes   □ No   □ Sometimes

4. Do you attend church now?

□ Yes   □ No   □ Sometimes

5. How would you best describe yourself BEFORE Alpha? (Check all that apply)

□ Searching   □ Spiritual, but no religious affiliation

□ Undecided   □ Christian

□ Skeptical   □ Other: _____

6. How would you best describe yourself NOW? (Check all that apply)

□ Still Searching   □ Spiritual, but no religious affiliation

□ Undecided   □ Christian

□ Skeptical   □ Other: _____

Guest Feedback Form

7. If the answers to questions 5 & 6 are different, when did the change occur?

❑ Alpha Weekend/Day

❑ Gradually over time

❑ Other:_____

Please describe your experience and any significant moments:

_____

_____

8. In what ways did you benefit from being a part of Alpha? (Check all that apply)

❑ Feel more at peace   ❑ Discovered a relationship with God through Jesus

❑ Strengthened my faith   ❑ Found new purpose for life

❑ Made new friends   ❑ Other: _____

❑ Feel more love/loved

9. On a scale of 1-5, how positive was your experience of the Alpha Weekend/Day
Circle best answer

(1 = not important; 5 = very important)

    1   2   3   4   5

10. Comments, suggestions, areas to improve:

_____

_____

_____

_____

Appendix H

Team Feedback Form

Name: _____   Date: _____
        (optional)

1. How did you get involved with Alpha?

_____

_____

_____

2. What was your role on the Alpha Team? (Check all that apply)

❒ Greeter   ❒ Food Prep Team

❒ Small Group Host   ❒ Worship Team

❒ Small Group Helper   ❒ Alpha Weekend/Day Team

❒ Set-up/ Takedown Team   ❒ Other: _____

3. How many times have you helped on the Alpha team? _____

4. Which Alpha Training session(s) did you participate in? (Check all that apply)

❒ Small Groups

❒ Prayer & the Weekend

❒ I did not attend any Alpha Training sessions

5. What was most helpful about the training?

_____

_____

Team Feedback Form

6. **In what ways did you benefit from serving on the Alpha team? (Check all that apply)**

☐ Used my gifts & skills   ☐ Met new people & made new friends

☐ Relied more on God   ☐ Learned how to run a small group discussion

☐ Experienced God myself   ☐ Witnessed God at work in people's lives

☐ Enjoyed being part of a team   ☐ Other: _____

7. **What did you find challenging about serving on the Alpha team?**

_____

_____

_____

8. **If you attended the Alpha Weekend/Day, please rate the following (1 = Poor, 5 = Excellent)**

Location	_____	Small Group Time	_____
Facilities	_____	Prayer Time	_____
Meals	_____	Fun/Free Time	_____
Alpha Talks	_____	Cost	_____

9. **Are you interested in being a part of the Alpha team again?**

Yes / No

10. **If yes, in which area(s) would you most like to serve?**

1. _____

2. _____

3. _____

What is Alpha?

Alpha is a series of sessions exploring the Christian faith, typically run over eleven weeks. Each talk looks at a different question around faith and is designed to create conversation. Alpha is run all around the world, and everyone is welcome.

Find out more

alphausa.org | alphacanada.org | caribbean.alpha.org

"Alpha was the best thing I ever did. It helped answer some huge questions and find a simple, empowering faith in my life."
Bear Grylls, Adventurer

Global Alpha Stats

169 countries | over 30 million guests | 81 languages

What to expect
A typical Alpha

Alpha runs in cafés, churches, universities, homes, bars—you name it. No two Alphas look the same, but they generally have three key things in common: food, a talk and good conversation.

Alpha Topics

Alpha explores the following topics over 11 weeks, including a weekend or day away. We recommend beginning and ending each Alpha with a party where guests can invite their friends who might be interested in attending the next Alpha. Alpha is free of charge to guests.

Session 1:   Is There More to Life Than This?
Session 2:   Who is Jesus?
Session 3:   Why Did Jesus Die?
Session 4:   How Can I Have Faith?
Session 5:   Why and How Do I Pray?
Session 6:   Why and How Should I Read the Bible?
Session 7:   How Does God Guide Us?

Alpha Weekend or Day Away

Session 8:   Who is the Holy Spirit?
Session 9:   What Does the Holy Spirit Do?
Session 10:   How Can I Be Filled with the Holy Spirit?
Session 11:   How Can I Make the Most of the Rest of My Life?

Session 12:   How Can I Resist Evil?
Session 13:   Why and How Should I Tell Others?
Session 14:   Does God Heal Today?
Session 15:   What About the Church?

Getting started with Alpha

PREPARE: We're here to help you
We are eager to help you get your Alpha started. Contact us to connect with a network of experienced Alpha coaches and leaders in your local region.

PLAN: Go online to build your Alpha
Within Alpha Builder you will find team training videos and resources both for you and for your Alpha team. Oh, did we mention they are all free?

It's crucial that you make sure that all of your hosts, helpers and other team members are trained. Alpha small groups are different from other small groups that they may have participated in before, so they need to know how to run their group well.

PROMOTE: Easily promote your Alpha with our tools
Easily promote your Alpha by customizing our tools within Alpha Builder. You can post your Alpha on our website so guests can find you online. You can also download free resources to invite guests to your next Alpha. In the USA you can also find many promotional tools in our print shop at alpharesources.org.

PRAY: Lay the right foundation
Prayer is the foundation of Alpha. Gather a team to pray and go for it. You are part of a global story and we cannot wait to hear how it goes.

"What if I told you that Alpha is the most predictably redemptive tool I've ever seen in 40 years of ministry? Would you pilot one Alpha group in your church?"

Bill Hybels, Senior Pastor of Willow Creek Community Church

One Alpha, three ways to run

The Alpha Film Series
Begin the greatest adventure with us. The Alpha Film Series is an updated, relevant and engaging way to experience the Alpha talks. They are designed to take the audience on an epic journey exploring the basics of the Christian faith.

Alpha with Nicky Gumbel
Alpha pioneer Nicky Gumbel delivers a complete set of 29-minute Alpha talks for a new generation. Filmed live at HTB, London, Nicky Gumbel provides the timeless version of Alpha talks for tens of thousands of churches of all denominations around the world.

The Alpha Youth Series
Twelve video sessions filmed all around the globe, designed to engage students and young people in conversations about faith, life and Jesus. DVD available for purchase or online for free.

Related Alpha resources

Alpha Toolkit
The Alpha Toolkit will help you to plan and run your Alpha. It also provides training materials, the main talk videos, team and guest resources, and more.

Questions of Life
Questions of Life is the foundational teaching of Alpha. It is a step-by-step guide to the basics of the Christian faith by one of the world's most respected Christian leaders. This book explores key themes, questions and objections to faith, leading us on an engaging, personal journey of discovery.

Alpha Guide
Essential for every Alpha guest, the guide serves as a companion to the talks. The guide is an invaluable resource to guests during Alpha and as a reference for individual reflection long after Alpha is over.

Alpha Team Guide
This essential tool for Alpha small group hosts and helpers can be used with team training videos. It contains outlines for each training session as well as sample questions for hosting each session of Alpha.

Run Alpha Handbook
If you're planning to run Alpha, this handbook contains everything you need to know. These pages tell the story of Alpha and practically explain how to plan, prepare and promote your course. This guide will leave you fully equipped to manage your team, plan your sessions and run a great Alpha.

30 Days: A Practical Introduction to Reading the Bible
God has given humanity the extraordinary privilege of knowing him through his word. Nicky Gumbel has selected thirty fascinating passages from the Old and New Testament, accompanied by an insightful commentary and suggested prayer.

Marriage Courses
The Marriage Preparation and The Marriage Course can be run either before or after Alpha and are an excellent way to reach out to the wider community. The Marriage Courses are very easy to run; the talks are available on DVD and each guest and leader receives a manual. If you enjoy hosting people and have a passion for strengthening family life, you could run a course!

The Marriage Course
The Marriage Course is for any couple who wants to invest in their relationship, whether they have been together 1 or 61 years and whether they have a strong relationship or are struggling.

The Marriage Preparation Course
Most couples spend countless hours preparing for the wedding, but little, if any, time preparing for married life. The Marriage Preparation Course can help couples develop strong foundations for a lasting marriage.

**For more information in the USA,
visit alphausa.org/the-marriage-courses
or purchase materials at alpharesources.org.**

**For more information in Canada,
visit themarriagecourses.ca
or purchase the materials at parasource.com.**

Alpha USA
1635 Emerson Lane
Naperville, IL 60540

800.362.5742
+ 212.406.5269

info@alphausa.org
alphausa.org
alpharesources.org

@alphausa

Alpha in the Caribbean
Holy Trinity Brompton
Brompton Road
London SW7 1JA UK

+44 (0) 845.644.7544

americas@alpha.org
caribbean.Alpha.org

@AlphaCaribbean

Alpha Canada
Suite #230
11331 Coppersmith Way
Richmond, BC V7A 5J9

800.743.0899

office@alphacanada.org
alphacanada.org

Purchase resources in Canada:

Parasource Marketing & Distribution
Canada
P.O. Box 98, 55 Woodslee Avenue
Paris, ON N3L 3E5

800.263.2664

custserv@parasource.com
parasource.com

Printed in the USA
CPSIA information can be obtained
at www.ICGtesting.com
JSHW010926260624
65293JS00027B/11